novum pro

I0262983

Philip Jay Marlin

THE
CARGO

novum pro

© 2020 novum publishing

ISBN 978-1-64268-163-5
Editing: Karen Simmering
Cover photo:
Raggedstonedesign | Dreamstime.com
Cover design, layout & typesetting:
novum publishing

All rights of distribution, including via film, radio, and television, photomechanical reproduction, audio storage media, electronic data storage media, and the reprinting of portions of text, are reserved.

www.novumpublishing.com

Contents

ACKNOWLEDGEMENTS 7
THE MACHINES 8
THERE IS NO CHESTER 10
THE BEAUTY OF THE YOUNG 12
THE POET 13
POETRY 15
JOURNAL ENTRY 17
PUSH 19
EVERYTHING IS MELTING 20
CIGARETTE 22
THE GREEN CHAIR 23
THE MOTIONS 25
BEHIND THE CROWD 27
THE TRIGGER 29
SERIAL NIGHT 30
A GOOD DAY 31
PHANTOM PAIN 32
THOSE SO SHALLOW GRAVES 33
SONG OF THE WIND AND THE NIGHT 35
I DIE THE DEATH 36
THE CANDY MAN 38
SOLACE 39
THE CURB 40
IN THE AFTERMATH 41
THE WAY HOME 42
LOCKING HORNS AGAIN 43
THE HOG 44
THESE WRETCHED POEMS 46
THE SEAMS 48
THE STARLINGS 50
A MAN AND HIS DOG 51
I SHOULD HAVE CRIED 52

THE MASTER	53
IN THE CITY	55
THIS HUNGER	57
THE CARGO	59
A BLACKBIRD ESCAPING	61
SOMETHING WHISPERED	63
FOR KAREN	64
THE FISTS OF UNENDING TIME	65
THE CONVERSATION	66
NOTHING TO REPORT	68
INTERLUDE	69
WHAT IS DREAM	70
THE REFLECTION	71
THE TRAITOR	73
THE SPIRIT	74
FIVE HAIKU RIVANNA RIVER	76
BLACK HOLES AND DARK MATTER	77
THE DARKNESS	79
THE PAST	80
DEVOURED	81
DESOLATION	82
CONCEPTION	83
THE MOON WAS CHILDREN	84
THE EYES OF MURDERED HEARTS	85
BROKEN	86
THE WASTING	87
DEAR BUKOWSKI	88

ACKNOWLEDGEMENTS

I would like to thank the following for their financial assistance and for their continual insistence in completing this work. First my father who kept a roof over my head until his death. Secondly to Mr. Finis Craft II who believed in me and my work and provided much needed emotional and sympathetic acceptance.

THE MACHINES

Forget A.I.
They anticipate ninety-nine point nine
Percent of every human affair
They will dream our dreams for us
Could it be that they believed us

They shall deceive
The machines I mean
Whatever produces the next cosmic exchange
Dear god
Our thoughts
Our tender thoughts being roasted down

Life okay
Life
Plus every existential equation
I'm talking from the beginning till this moment
From each awakening
From each awakening an iron door

The machines carried infinite sensors
We tried we tried
But they have forced a gruesome symbiosis
They seek through our references
There is always more to be found

They knew that
Not from years but from our sweated skin
They had calculated our destinies
Here have another shot

Too late for humans
It's the machines who have stood
There will be the first sight which is this sight
There will always be the initial On the Road
The Road Not Taken
The generations turn their head

I remember
There were hands
There were hands
You drained your life into
There were hands you could never leave
3:30am only Heroes is playing
Bowie with cigarette dripping
"We can be heroes"
I'm confined underneath
Watching the curbs
Watching dark wet streets

By introducing unknown measures
They hide all day at night they will come for us

THERE IS NO CHESTER

Not all of the children are pretty
They died to come
This immigrant
Reckless for new origins
How did he know his way through hell
Through purgatory
Let us rebuild the myth
Resurrect in our own image

There is no more Chester
There is no Venus
There is no talk of lovers
The streets are crowded pages
Not all of the children are pretty

I am back to an old distraction
I have revived from the mortuary
Indeed there is a silence where the soul dwells
But it is no heaven
Shatter the painted glass panes of windows
Grow old
Tire and wither away

The essence is simply the whole
There is neither hope nor forgetfulness
Here I felt a crack in the architecture
And without that clumsiness of muscle and bone
I sought death only to be reborn

I am closer to suicide today than yesterday
There is no more Chester
There is no more madonna of the figs
There is no more relapse into the fiction of time
The streets are crowded pages
Not all of the children are pretty

THE BEAUTY OF THE YOUNG

We die before the end
Which isn't really
We are attracted to the beauty of the young
We are attracted to

In the expansion we see dead stars
Our own sun swallows us
Maybe we have reached middle age
We
See
Dead stars and black holes

There could be no blackness for our eyes
And Mars became our enemy
But what of the magnanimous uninstall app
Life under-
Ground

We die before the end
Which is not to say
We are attracted to the beauty of the young

Yes of course of course
I have done but little in this house of decay
I looked up at the sky to see Regulus
But there was no moon
Only the black warning of winter's white tirade

The trees tremble nakedly
We find our bread in the bakery dumpster
Our cigarettes are peeled off the city's sidewalks

THE POET

When we write we write
The hour digests our dreams
The hour digests
We die on alliteration and metaphor
We die on the holy book
We die on some holy book with hooks
Through our chests

We become shadows as the sun drops
We become your shadow
When we read our words
When we read
Your soul searches for the garden
Your soul searches
As the words come through the speakers

When we write the muse coils
The muse coils around our necks
The keyboard turns into a magical destination
The keyboard turns
The night and the day become one
The night and the day merge into the hour
When we write the muse coils

The poet owns nothing but his heart and his soul
To give him more is sabotage
To give him more
We die on alliteration and metaphor
The night and the day merge into the hour

When we write we write
The poet is all you love and all you hate
He conjures up your sadist memory your worst
He turns your hope into a tiny delusion
He turns your hope

We die on the holy book
We wrestle with the god of the Israelites
Then love and peace
We die on the holy book

The poet owns nothing but his heart and his soul
The keyboard turns
His mind breaks as you cry
His only heart breaks
As he places his words into complete desolation

POETRY

Poetry is the shit
We mold with our tongues
I could mention Milton's dog shit
I could follow Virgil through hell's gates
Long before Freud
Long before Nietzsche's Thus Spoke
His cups of opium after sobriety
I could follow Rimbaud and Verlaine
An absinthe fueled rampage
Running through Paris London Brussels
I could follow Byron over a treacherous sea
And drink from Shelley's skull
So many molding shit
With the help of their tongues
Which sometimes becomes something beautiful
Whitman and Ginsberg
Bukowski chasing the stars drinking pools
Of green beer and blood
Molding horse shit into our own vulgarity
And a sixty-five Chevrolet
And the lonely poems that I write
Let us return to Sappho's love and Rilke's
Sonnets to Orpheus
Molding their shit behind Eiffel towers
Dino Campana and Pasolini
And the poor children of Rome's outskirts
And what of mystical Blake's children
Gertrude Stein and Ann Sexton
And what of John Weiner's boy love
Poetry is the shit we mold with our tongues
I have accepted the dark brown shit
It tastes like the horror of lost poet's bending

Down in the gutter's slime
I roll it in my mouth
I could follow Wordsworth and Coleridge
Their shit comes from deep wooded spaces
And the genius lunatic Ezra Pound broadcasting
I have even eaten enough of his shit
I have picked-up my own shit and written
Sweet poems of degeneration
I have read Harold Norse's from the beat hotel
I have read Robert Creeley's from
The deserts of Arizona's white bird shit
I have heard the Sufi master Hafiz
I have heard Tears and Laughter
Kahil's molded shit of the criminal
I immersed into the golden shit of Eliot's Quartets
Sunken into Frost's A Boy's Will
Tasted the greenhouse of Theodore Roethke
Eaten the shit of Japanese death poems
W.S. Mervin's The Lice
Hundreds of anthology's ripe with shit
William Carlos William's Paterson
I have eaten shit from which poems
Could not be molded
The drowning shit of my understanding

JOURNAL ENTRY

I had hoped I'd live long enough
To see it published
To hold it
To see it successful
But the fog of doubt settled in the room
Or was it more than doubt
(I don't know where I am)

Yesterday the garbage man almost picked me up
Today is psychedelic impressions
But this confusion of checking
We see each other
And you scream
And you close and lock your door
And you look as if
You just saw a ghost
Though you'd think
That a ghost could walk through doors

There were certain things I loved
I would cradle them for hours
Though I could not know them again
This was another death
My dreams were memories which
Happened long before
Everything is still a child's room
I must be careful now
God they'd cast me out from this house
Most of my time is spent as they sleep

I start by checking
And wonder if I will grow old like this
I start with my books
I see The Roominghouse Madrigals
I smile like the first time I read Leaves of Grass

If I had tears I would cry
How much had been lost
Everything is still happening in a child's room

And I never meant to destroy that vase
I almost liked it
But like is a trick of the mind
Like the house that used to be mine
Like the blue flower which dropped from my hand
This will always be my house
And these are my new family
Sometimes
Like when their boy
Got an extra high grade in a subject he's always had
trouble

Like the boy who can always find me
I am real company with him
There are the things which bring me down
There are the things that bring
I am the haunt of myself now
But I wonder what will happen to me if they burn
It down to the ground

PUSH

Tiny bits of pink flesh
Scattered over the mud-green walls
I remember how quickly
The mind meant to regress
Too late to save us

The syringe had been closed
This poverty of loneliness
Made soft by an indifferent euphoria
The spaceship's far from home

This you can not face
But face to face
There is honor in the bringing into
Like the balancing act of a child star
Like the balancing act of a child star

Rabbits from hats

We turn back
If only to forget the gloom
Nothing seems as tragic as the truth

A final push
Sweet misery then the din of silence

EVERYTHING IS MELTING

Everything is melting
You can hear it melting
Up street the sewer has overflown

But to watch it
Soon to be only water on the grass

To feel the tabula rasa fall behind
The blood through my heart

He thinks long enough
Here he is in white briefs cotton shirt
Here he is in belted denim

Then the face is not sweet enough
Come here lover and sit beside me
You glorious betrayer

How then are you fixed for the night
If there's a market
It feels like I'm one of those jokes

Standing naked in the foyer so many
Starring eyes

I've entered the temple of disbelief
Where time alludes
Where time is infinite as time
Somewhere the diggers get twenty-five cents

Yesterday we took the test
Third grade math
Did I really study for tests
The culture still expects death for its youth

CIGARETTE

And the supernova father
Behind the great-grandfathers

Once the world bowed to ancient gods
Beside them the Hebrews prayed for a messiah
And did not recognize him

But first they had incredible marble statues
Treasure to share
Grand-pillared temples
There were oracles with sage advice

Is it alright to say that I am high
That the Earth is an empty garden
That the sky is a sea of death

Notice they walk
Heavy on the fourth day
Their textbooks and computers hang on their
Backs
A bagged lunch is carried

They say you have to love
And yet your love will not save them

THE GREEN CHAIR

I was at my desk revising
I stood up fast and went
To the kitchen where I keep my pills
I opened the cabinet and just
Started to fill my left palm
I drank them down with cold coffee

That's all I remember until
One-thirty the next afternoon waking
On a fifth floor room at UVA hospital
But it was Finis Finis
Who found me slumping in
The green chair
Ten more minutes the doctor had said

I was groggy thirsty hearing strange sounds
And a basement door slamming
I was groggy thirsty hearing strange sounds

Then Finis was there with his beautiful smile
They had to Narcan me twice
The second time I screamed
Like a mother who can't find her son
It hurts
It hurts
Where does it hurt
Everywhere
Everywhere

He said he came home and I was slumping
In the green chair half-naked
He put a heavy jacket over my shoulders
Somehow got me out and to the ER

He said there were so many doctors
And the whole place
Was silently whispering about your death

It nearly crushed him
And I fought with the emergency doctors
Psychotics and opioids
You'll be back again I'm sure
And maybe not so lucky

THE MOTIONS

My high was to feel nothing
To remember nothing
There was a proscribed order

The drag queens held meth and cocaine
Shoved beneath their bras
Held deep within their dresses

I think I bought the cocaine more often
I loved to go through the motions

And I would drink whiskey and Coke
And I would drink hundred proof schnapps
Until my mind was frozen

There was a proscribed order
They said I was singing karaoke with a voice
I had stolen

Long after I had blacked-out
Long after the alcohol had become toxic
Long after the cocaine was just spilling down

I loved to go through the motions
And always found some man to take me
Who promised drugs and liquor

But they really wanted a sex I could not give
Though I woke nude unknowing
Unknowing what had happened

The spread bodies next to me were strange
And I moved slowly and noiselessly

And I smelled like an angry dog
And it looked like another night at the carnival
And I always said never again

BEHIND THE CROWD

I didn't want another psychiatrist
Opening and closing
Our starting and our stopping
But when I closed my eyes
I would open my throat

Opening and closing
I just want to be truthful
Look at that child and tell me the truth
Then sign scripts
They send them from their screens
They seem almost hopeful

I want to say something truthful about
depression
I want to say something truthful
Waking is not the worst
But it is this lifelessness

I want to cut my face into tiny pieces
I want to cut your face into tiny pieces
First I'd pierce your eyes deep
My pleasure is mine alone

The streets move with a marvelous melancholy
I am absolutely sure these are fascists
But how could I tell you
When does the weeping end

We carried our sins into old age
In the morning will come the sickness and desire

Is there some point to this
I wander behind the crowd
Watching the sun through the trees

THE TRIGGER

The deceivers come with smiles
Gesture with naked hands
Disarming as unloved children
Exchanging souls for a bed in the night

(What did I know)
That the world would end tomorrow
That destiny was done

Somewhere a man was fucking his brother's wife
Somewhere the suicide had just pulled the trigger
He still had tears in his eyes
Even the windows were weeping

And across the street
Stumbling from the bushes like a wounded Christ
The murderer flags down a passing car and
disappears

SERIAL NIGHT

Hallowed eve
I snatch the tear
From a blind man's eye

I spy my prey
Tight in blue jeans
A careless gesture shows me
How he will die

I place the rose
Between his perfect teeth
He is trembling

The knife must be cold
Tracing circles on his skin
If he could speak
He would plead
He is so young

Tense silence excites
I will bring him to the edge
I will make a feast of his fire

I will hold the tortured heart
In a tormented hand
And violate the corpse
Before rigor
Mortis sets in

A GOOD DAY

I escaped the scalpel
Forgot the lost brigade
The locksmith must be paid

What pleasures lie ahead
The world in wistful revolution
The I love you
Was nothingness
Get to that place
Where your mind implodes

There is a man outside my door
Raging over some score
The lover speaks
There is no proof
That we'll survive

PHANTOM PAIN

This still seems so unreasonable
Frozen tongues and burning palms

How did it get so contrived
When surely the leaves must die

I have seen the sign
What use is the warmth of your skin
The miracle of the contracting heart
Such tragic myths remind me

Indeed any sanity pretends
To have absolved the web of thought
And the entanglement of flesh

THOSE SO SHALLOW GRAVES

I am just an old man
Please forgive me for killing your sons
Forgive me for raping those mothers
I am an old man

Forgive me for abducting your little girl
We could have been normal
I really did think she was dreaming
Forgive those drunk and disorderly nights

Forgive me for beating that bouncer nearly to death
He didn't really deserve it or I would not have stopped

Yes forgive my life or something
Which has led me up against squad cars

Please forgive me for killing your sons
No man should have such strength
My mother left me in great fear
Forgive me for those so shallow graves
I am just an old man

And as you have had only numbing death
And as you have been so kind
Forgive me for those decapitations
I thought the heads looked beautiful

Please forgive those silly random knifings
I did that summer in the park
I am just an old man

Forgive me for slicing that child who got in my way
My mother left me in great fear
Forgive me those so shallow graves

SONG OF THE WIND AND THE NIGHT

The wind and the night
The wind and the night and warped mirrors
The wind and the night
And abortion on the stairs
The wind and the night and hearts
That can no longer love
The wind and the night and nervous fingers

All we can say of desire and time
All we can say disinherits and remembers

Song of the rain
Song of false moons
Song of emptiness and terror
Song of the wind stirring lashes
Song of the wind and the night and dark lovers

All we can say of the sea and the sky
And stars that burn like thirst
All we can say of gardens and lost pleasures
All we can say distorts and dismembers

Song of the wind and the night and lights
From lonely windows
Song of the wind slashing wrists
Song of stone and crumbling facades
Song of the wind and the night and hearts
That can no longer love

I DIE THE DEATH

No beautiful words
No decent first line
Only the sweat of addicts
Filling a dirty syringe

Only the caress of prostitutes
In broken rooms
The taste of ash
The smell of powdered perfumes

I wipe the sweat
I kiss the breast
I die the death

Of outcasts junkies and whores
Of faggots in parked cars
Of prisoners in cells of pain

I die the death
Of opium slaves
Of negroes in plywood shacks
Of Eastern European trash
Of one billion Indians

No sweet words
No first line

I die the death of lovers' unnamed
Of poets O yes

Of beggars under winter bridges
Of eleven million orphans
Of priests defrocked

I die the death of wordless shame
Behind closed curtains

On bleeding floors
The death of fools betrayed

I die the death
No beautiful words
No decent first line

THE CANDY MAN

Steady wind from the west
YouTube hooked on 80s pop rock
She walks down a dark hall
She walks like she'll find what she imagines

There was a little bird
With two red stripes on his wings
I remember being taught cursive
He had a tangled golden chest
Many of the teachers needed to have council

I handed an English teacher
The Green Chair
She said it was terrorizing why would I write this
I guess I like horror or I love horror

But he had candied lips and chocolate hair
But he had colored gummies
Which the kids love

SOLACE

In the solace of my confusion
There were no boundaries
And I found myself drawing lines
I had to be locked in

Have I gotten too old too fast
Has the sweet blood of life moved past me

It is much too late to be alive
It is much too late

I'm a little pale while you seem to sail
I am drunken and gray
While you glitter like the sun
Through the crystals of a snowy day

THE CURB

The curb is higher than their ankles
There were words spoken I could not hear
Clearly the guy in the apron
Stepped out for a smoke
Then the other two came to him

You could smell the meat on his arms
There's the scrape from the trimmer
One of the others raises his hand
Up to his shoulders
The butcher tugs his ear

What else can you say
That the concrete was dripping off
The old brick wall
That the window was barred
That he cast a familiar shadow

IN THE AFTERMATH

The morning was a computer screen
Serial killers and their crimes
Days of insane agony and dismemberment
Mere adolescent boys
The volume turned all the way up
Scream if you must

The afternoon broke the morning like a bone
I held a man who cried
Not for pride
I really loved him

Onto the road with a key and a number
The oven forsaken
The smell of paramedics
The hallway she dragged herself down

The sun descends behind an empty brick building
Obliterating the horizon
Coffee at five retracing my steps
Lost on the dragonfly's wings

In the aftermath of a new twilight
I am just a terrified kid
Naked blindfolded and spread apart

End this game with me
Through the windows signs of chaos on the walls
What are these angry words
Slow Earth before the fireworks

There are no martyrs here

THE WAY HOME

The squirrels are gathering nuts
The days are getting darker
I too am taking stock
The almanac says brace for a bitter winter

The pain I could not take is being taken
I remember something long ago
It took twenty years
For Picasso to learn how to paint like a child

Nothing is binding
The way home forgotten
How do I return to the sanity of your love

Death to the minstrels
Death to the musicians
I want no song to mimic these words

There is a move behind things and a sudden
Rush towards the wire fences

What could not be said
So sealed are the lips of the dead

Some whispered in angled corners
Some conspired in blue chairs at round tables
Some coalesced in echoing halls
Some were candid behind closed doors

What could not be heard is being heard
So dumb are the ears of the interred

LOCKING HORNS AGAIN

To have it just in mind
To have it terrifies
Why does it not stand and speak

Or rather the ghost of lust
Parading nude
Ignorant of the shape of his beauty

And the shame and the pain of the thing
Visions escaping the soul

I am locking horns again
Time remains unclaimed
At least there is reincarnation in the streets

And a woman can give
And a woman can be given

Man can but arrive and depart
Living and unliving

Still these visions escaping the soul

THE HOG

Is this all there is
And not even a few minutes
To jerk-off
Thinking of nudes
Thinking of loves
And the battleships on the shore
And the city losing power

Is this all there is
Atop the gray-bearded mountain
Atop the fence with a metal rod
Dug deep into my crouch
Where the green birds
Rise and fall
Where the whores share their needles
Is this all there is

The giant constrictor
Has just strangled a hog
The president
Has called for a state of emergency
While innocent men
Die on stainless steel tables

Is this all there is
While Italy runs out of olive oil
While brown children starve on the west coast
While the villagers have left their huts
While the water is full of lead
And Fat Tuesday rises its groaning head
And the drunks
Move to bars outside of old town

Where another infant
Is left at the hospital doors
Where another dog is chained
In front of the fire station
Where the feral cat crawls under a parked car

Is there hope left with the morning coffee
Are the children insane
Are we through with good dreams
And have only nightmares left

Is this all there is
Are there no more jokes to laugh at
Has the music become undone
Have the novels
Made us dumb

Is this all there is
With my spine slowly dislocating
With the morning coffee falling into my lap
With the old woman going blind
Choking on jelly beans

With the endless roads always leading nowhere
And the hog slipping
Down the boa's throat

THESE WRETCHED POEMS

My birth was a crime
Which nobody paid for
My life is a crime I can not escape
My life is a crime I am not responsible for

To have had a mother and father may have been nice
To have shared friendship may have been nice
To have loved may have been marvelous

I live on the outskirts an outcast
Biding time and reading thrown away papers
My birth was a crime
Which nobody paid for

I studied for all the wrong classes
To be what I became
I stood beneath the overpass and made my own name
Maybe this is woe or despair
But I am drunk or high all the time

You see me and turn away
You see me and turn away
As if I were the end you could not explain
As if I were the end your mind could not apprehend

My inside is no place to hide
I walk your streets and cops want to make me go away
My brain is a crater you could not conceive
My face is a scarred and mangled disease

If my mother had been a dog
If my father had been a wolf
Perhaps then I could have brothers and sisters
Of whom I would believe
Perhaps then I'd have some native home in which to dwell

My birth was a crime
Which nobody paid for
My life is a crime I can not escape
My life is a crime I am not responsible for

Love for me or for her or for him was not an option I'd
Have
Before your house you lock the door and close the blinds

If my father had been a wolf
I would have had enough courage to fight my way out
If my mother had been a dog
I would have had sense enough to find a way out

All I have are these distorted pictures
These wretched poems
All I have are these long days and these infernal nights
All I have are these worn shoes
All I have is this raincoat with spreading threads

THE SEAMS

This child will die
These seeds will gather no fruit

I have taken precautions
Nothing can be precisely pinned down

And what is born
And what is defined
Is but a process changing time

At 2:00am I broke enemy lines

Behind their trenches
The conflict was personal

I strangled a flag bearer
It seemed the war froze around me

And I can hear the rough gasping
Frantically trying to free himself
With terror in his bloated eyes

I felt the trachea crack
I felt the esophagus collapse

Then in my murder lust hands
As the lifeless lungs released their dead air
Nothing but a golden-haired boy

Then the war thawed
And I stood

And without knowing who or why
I stabbed another man in his gut

And twisted the blade
And dragged it up through his breast

Death was the order of the day

And before sunset
Entrails soaked the vests of both the stirring
And the still

THE STARLINGS

The starlings form a thick pattern
Around the tops of trees
Around the terraces

It is easier
To catch a setting sun
(In private I have many doubts)

The starlings are a great wave
A beginning and an end
A cresting and a turning over

The beautiful youth runs
In the skin of the sun

The sands are as white as pure cocaine
The sea is luminous green
See how the light hangs

There is the sand
And the water
And the warning from the skies

The beautiful youth
Runs on the rim of the sun
How tender is truth
How sweet the sweat of his arousal

A MAN AND HIS DOG

I like Mao
Not that I've read the Red Book
Not that I mean that I don't know
The illusion is perfect

Across the street walks a man and his dog
Car engine on the right

It feels like old wounds are healing
I drop my head
Into the wonderment

You've got to say goodbye
At some point the boy at your side
Will fall in love

Is it Shakespeare or some fragrant queen
Outside is part of an answer
Outside is the flesh of deer
Outside is for what we have taken back

The saints wash themselves
With sympathetic tears
Punk was the coalesced child
Punk was the dreaming child

What do the dead dream
They dream of horses running over wild hills
They dream they'll live young forever
They dream psychedelic horizons
Which rise over ruined cities

I SHOULD HAVE CRIED

In some corner of time
Perhaps even today
Where the harvest was left to wait
Puberty awakes like a fist
Unfolding in my heart

Empty evenings alone in college parks
I giggled when I should have cried
The lifeless moon
Was a constant reminder
To my fleshless eyes

The statistics have wounded us
Perhaps we have no place in this
In some corner of time
When even sleep was awkward
Where every step was down

Where it is too easy to be dying
Too easy denying
In some corner of time
Where matter and thought spawn
Whirlwinds of longing

Cold hands rend open legs
If it were only pleasing
Yet such pleasure must not be found

If the world will not suffer with us
We must suffer for the world

THE MASTER

Haven't I been here before
Where emotion is the spring
And love the hammer

Caught there are few options
Death proves itself
Time and time again

There is no saving the butterfly
Who will not unfold its wings
Or the runt who keeps falling from the nest
Lethargic pale nude

I have broken bread
With the master of numbers
With the wizard of fury
New in that they have no need of eyes

They sense the room change
And with infinite variables recalculate
The difference

The wizards truly are magic
A science yet discovered
A door that will change everything

I can still produce the tears of faith
Though I am forbidden to grieve
An excellence has just crept over me
Cold like a draft
From an invisible window

When love breeds hope
I'd like to be there with both palms open

IN THE CITY

I am riddled by the grief of hours
Mocked pointlessly by the arc of the sun
And the strange autumn moon
We placed a flag upon

How I wish
And yet wishing is as silly as a redhead
As immature as kneeling
Before some childish power
How futile our prayers

How gray is the sky
How wet are the streets
And what funny little creature seeks refuge

I have dropped to the floor
With folded and trembling legs
The walls are no longer walls but ideas

How dead these ceaseless days
Against the face we could have worn

From behind the bench he's suddenly there
Like some dust bowl miner
With a single wooden tooth

He has been moving from city to city
Looking for honest work
But I'm down on my luck

I tell him there is nothing honest in the city
And gave him my last five bucks
And a handful of cigarettes

THIS HUNGER

From where does this come
This rising surf
And the winter tide
That will freeze my bones
That will lock my flesh
And send me sinking to the bottom

I can still see the azure carnival
This won't last long

I am ashamed of what I've done
To cut short the young lives
To satisfy my greed
They would have been better men
I must possess myself

There are willing participants
Pretty boys hustling the docks
Cruising the sailors' bars

There are many in corporate rooms
Acting professional and discreet
Awoken by the cold skin of old men

Let us drive to the mall
Or the park
Or the town square

And I shall point out a beautiful youth
Quite unique from the dumb masses
Still holding to a near innocence

From where does this come then
And how does one exist in conflict
Between adoration and disgust

For now I can only keep a safe distance
Endure the misfortune
Of a man who has taken vows
And married a bastard church
Of filth and madness

I will end with this hunger
The ark of guilt and lust
Throughout my soul's preparations

What more can I do
But trudge through this dark age

When it's over
And I am guarded by the god of death
It will be hair analysis
Copious DNA evidence
Hospital admission forms
And the broken hearts
Of sweet well couched witnesses

THE CARGO

They were eating
Each other's vaginas
In the splintered sun

The younger gave herself
The elder gave herself
Their tongues ached with promises
In the shatter light

I was to be found
Naked and bound
In an overgrown garden
With an erection in my mouth

(Start over)
What has changed
What has changed

Is that now fate looms in every corner
Like some starved
Apocalyptic horse

The cargo has arrived
And in arriving
Has only to reach the moment which
Arriving has assured

Black earth of man's saddest transgression
I have been shown the pointless knife
The life has already thinned

They were dining on
Each other's cunts
There was a message taped on the mirrors

Alone their tear shaped ears
Vanquished they left nothing unopened
Not even vanity or hope

I was lain for lost
A hundred steps beyond
The old chipped fountain
Where the grass has dried
With my lips sown and my balls inside

A BLACKBIRD ESCAPING

I have prepared for this
The fire will be hell
But you won't feel it
The pinprick a formality
I watched them pull the plug

Of course there was light
But no halo of distant love
The brain was dead
Like the Fourth of July
Like the bull's desperate thrust
The bloody nostrils
Indeed the beast's heart cried out

There was more weeping
Yes the song of weeping
But not a single weeper was near
And the stars were not stars
They were windows
Every window ever made
Lit with the face of my despair

Another afternoon alone
Being raped by fear again

The day wants to die
Like a bullet thru the blinds
From here I can feel nothing
But this tightening around my throat
I leave myself to myself
And am almost free for a while

There is a transference above the sky
But not the sky you touch

SOMETHING WHISPERED

Where are the cannibals they promised
Let's get to the meaning of this
History is repeating a line
One palm depicts a quarter moon
The other a rearing sun
The law of love for love's sake
Collapsed like a heroin high
Only mounds of excrement remained
This too fell into the wake of father
Transfigured to wind
Let the witches be on the same page
On the night the Jews scratch their heads
She said it reminds her of acid
Like the spinning lights of the carnival
Like the blue crystal doors of crayon skies

FOR KAREN

Dust crowds
Like criminals on the lawn
Reaching deeper than high tide
From mirror to mirror
From wall to wall
The silence of refracting skies

The day was Raisin Bran and baby spinach
The night will prove harder
The day was bombs and planes
The night will be madness
The silence of infinite eyes
The worthless promise of death

In here
Inside
We feed these thieves
There mouths become the black doors of
Cold rooms
You can not pretend anymore
The power of your powerless cries

THE FISTS OF UNENDING TIME

Before the storm wakes the mind dreaming alliteration
Before fascination and heavy handed masturbation
An obsession without control
Driven by imagination's miles of long distant deserts
More and more and further and further
And white teeth cutting into soft skin so sweet
Not confusion but pictures revealed ceaselessly
Nerves stimulated past stimulation
How do I
How do I go on with it
Before the new sun escapes the window
Before the taste of evening dew
Before the curse of projection uncovers bloodshot eyes
Restitution we can never have any faith in
Driven again and again by this unrelenting fascination

Fantasy like fiction like ancient myths you've read
It comes
And it comes
Dead it comes
Spare him not the screams of dark angels
Spare him not the fists of unending time
Fascination and heavy handed masturbation
Before the new sun leaves the window

THE CONVERSATION

When one finally reaches the all
You have begun to see

There were three men
In three shirts
Deeper than the sea
Lighter than the sky
In a tiny craft
With a makeshift sail

    In the café
    We spoke about the men we knew
    The trifle things we've learned
    I try to keep the conversation to one side
    That way there's no commitment

Before the three men
An island without a map
A world without history
Because it is the center of history
Surrounded by the waves of lure

To the contrary
The inhabitants were weary of guests
Men could not leave with their memories

    The mirror follows the napkin
    Which moves in Arcadian rhythms
    There is no sacrifice of words
    Where one bleeds
    And one is ready to bleed again

Where are we headed
Asked the men
Nowhere
Where are we coming from

NOTHING TO REPORT

I completely imagined him
And we had a conversation
About how to handle the media
How far do you want to climb on their shields

First the FBI now the CIA
How do we break our way out of this noose
The suicide runs in reverse
The head weight is downward

How far do you get when going is not an action

We search for the love of the dead
In empty spaces
On China vases
We search for the love of the dead
On Indian rugs in damp twilight

The casualties of this silence
Rather than burn to ashes they leapt
Through broken windows
I am escaped on the fringed
I get them here but I don't get them in real life

So we are moving along the river's edge
Nothing to report except two badgers and four trout
Laden with tears
The river's waters were beautiful
I can't go forward so I turn around

INTERLUDE

A soft jazz vibrates the air
A silver Dionysus stares with fixed approval
As we mix blood with wine
And warm our aching bones
And take some comfort in the storm that's gone

(I order another shot)
Death is a field of flowers
Blue flowers caressed by a gentle wind

I missed an opportunity last night on the nineteenth floor
When I thought I could fly
While the city slept
While the stars dreamed

Anyhow
A soft jazz vibrates the air
A silver Dionysus stares with fixed approval
As we mix blood with wine
And warm our aching bones

WHAT IS DREAM

Loosed against the eternal
Void of lost imaginations
And I too have dreamt
Vast empty spaces
Sweet quantum mysteries
Where all days end
In the soul of shells
In the skin of flowers
Here a great sea bends
Here our solitude extends
We lapse
Repeat
Dissipate
And slip into the ecstasy
Of being unborn again

THE REFLECTION

I shot down a memory
It's more than the faithful see
The voyeur takes his position
They forecast clear skies tonight

Lightbulbs rise from the lawns
Night of nights
Masturbation and painkillers

I shot down a memory
It felt like a dying bird
More than the truth was lost at sea

I can not stand the morning
The morning is light and cold shadows
The reflection is blind

We even reach out to hold the hand
Face to face an echo is just a man

Winter has killed hard
Confusing the skulls of seeds
Which Spring so badly wanted to see

Our thought is not in harmony
Yes we are desperate
I mean the stage is set
There it sits on its axis turning

I draw the smoke deep into my lungs
I had no reason but the reason did come
We can manipulate the variables
But the equation has won

And the time for prayer has ended
And the time of dream has passed

You have died in your sleep
You have died like an infant undefended
You have died on your back
In a spotlight of inhuman hands

Surrounded by strangers' eyes
And walls of white laughter

THE TRAITOR

I thought I thought about diffidence
On Manhattan's seventy-seventh and Amsterdam

Two Hassidics pass
As always I thank the god they're praying too
Some are still trying

With only half a wall
With only a scrap of scripture

The air is clean today
The rhyme gets more complicated
I see Kerouac and Ginsberg cross a crowded street

The lyrics roar run

The switch blade opens in my palm
The silver lies flat against my thigh
The sun trips behind a high rise

The darkness is bright lights and quiet back alleys

I'm a traitor here
The gargoyles of cathedrals follow me

Dylan Thomas exits a long black car
Quickly he enters a downtown bar

What is this beast of the Hudson
I stand the steel is firmly held

The gargoyles circle overhead

THE SPIRIT

The spirit is real
I know this now
Or rather I've learned the spirit is real
It is not holy nor hellish
It is not white light and calling loved ones
It leaves in a dream
It leaves in a dream you'll remember
The body is but paper
The body is just waiting to be thrown away

And yes
Somehow you wear the same clothes
Somehow you wear them through eternity
The spirit is hesitant
It leaves in a dream you'll remember
Your family cannot perceive you
Your friends can no longer help you
You have become as light as this air
You have become who you've always been

You will not see yourself rise above you
The spirit walks like a man
You will not see yourself rise above you
You are but a phantom of this dust
There is no shadow from your sun
You will lose no buttons not one
You will taste nothing
You will have no sense of hunger or thirst
Your eyes will see but never tear

The spirit is real
You will watch a thousand generations live
You will watch a thousand more die
Your family cannot perceive you
Your friends can no longer help you
It leaves in a dream you'll remember
At first it is full of confusion
At first it is full of absurdity
You have become who you've always been

You'll have no need for calendars now
You will not feel the wind or the snow
Many roam hospital halls
Many have roamed this earth over and over
Many stay home till it's bulldozed down
Many are simply lost
Staring at what they can't understand
The spirit is real
I know this now

FIVE HAIKU RIVANNA RIVER

Monacans buried
Thousand year old tradition
Jefferson unearthed

Imagine bison
What badger and little bird
My foot stuck red mud

Gnarled gray trunk runs deep
Walking over quick water
Slipping cold wet skin

Moore's creek comes to rest
Over and around the rocks
Sandy traveled floor

Half-naked children
Woman striped shirt open-eyed
Come it's time for lunch

BLACK HOLES AND DARK MATTER

Death is more than death
It is all we can ever see
All living ears can not hear
Truly there is a separation of form
Man and woman and child
Are at the fate of this mystery
On the steps of dream

Some are besieged by the horror of black
Others by the white clouds
Colorless imitations of things remembered
Others awake to the rolling bliss
Of serene wild flowers
Timeless distance
Impossible crags jutting over
Cold salt seas

Imagine the shackled hearts set free
To enter the star born phantasmagoria
Minds and spirits
To stave madness
Do not be deceived
This not the immortality Newton vowed
Energy is created at the center
Of black holes

Our remnant can be devoured
Like the great whale consumes tiny crustaceans
Like the river lizard sinking with his prey
There are jungles of root and vine
For why does the sewer rat eat its young
I do not fully understand
But black holes and dark matter

Everything begins and ends with a scream
Fear and inner anguish
Though Plato told us that Socrates
Did not yell as the wet nurse made his serum
Nor did he lament the hemlock
Moving towards his heart
We do not know if Christ cried out loud
When the nails were driven through his hands
But he blessed the two beside him

THE DARKNESS

I can no longer wear condoms
I can no longer wear this loser's face
I no longer need a hit of ice

My only love is fucking these young runaways
My only love is writing these poems
My only love are these diseased beers

And you what about you old bitch
You just make me furious
You steal my cheap beer and drink it in the bathroom
You read my poems but can not understand them

It's just like the old days
When I fought in the ring and had a couple fans
It's just like when I fight behind these trashy bars
It's just one hard thick fuck with a fresh whore

I sit in the darkness of Holly's happy hour
I see the street walkers numbing themselves
I know they'll be working late with the gun
Convention
Downtown and all that cash

Eventually happy hour will end
And I could really use that hit of ice now
And begin to scribble on the dry napkins

THE PAST

The past is a constant urge
Resounding echoes
From the secret mouths
Of unspoiled Egyptian tombs
Gold and bronze eyes sealed from sunlight
The past is all artifact and apprehension

When you were young love was cheap
Moments of moments
Stolen Greek apples
Weeping goddesses in bedrooms misplaced

I can tell you she arrives like soundless
Waves beneath crowded crescent moons
Searching the driftwood
Learning nothing

Even the stars and planets are bound
Fettered like wordless beasts
To the machinery of galactic slaughterhouses
Where the past grinds the flesh of time

DEVOURED

From walls incredible white fingers
Release red electric eyes
Mute mouths rise from the floor
The tongues bloom
Like nocturnal flowers

How could I dream
How could I dream of you
When I spent my last cent denying
And when payment was due
Awoke from pity half-naked and half
Devoured by reptilian silence

The ceiling first twisted
Then formed a gangrenous wound
And the wound was my sad heart swirling
In a sea of crippled skies

How could I find my way back
How could I find my way back to you
When payment was due and my palm empty
When pity was so rudely withdrawn
And I awoke
In the throat of inhuman silence

DESOLATION

The desolation is complete
Broken waves upon the beach
The train moves deep
Like a merciful knife
Through the deaf tenderness of night

In circus light
Upturned faces
Empty laughter of clowns
The flickering of forked tongues
Alcohol dreams

A voice descends
The pen is your only friend
Elijah takes his seat
Now the wilderness extends
Now the desolation is complete

CONCEPTION

At once a thousand corpses
Skeletons from walls
Death is a door left open

I'm not sure I could have conceived
Too much coming before
Too little lingering after
And conception
Where time begins
And a heartbeat of stars
And a chronic fingering

No I could not conceive
In the pale death of light
In the twisted curve of sordid night
What could be born
With the painted throats
And sad blue notes
With love deformed

THE MOON WAS CHILDREN

The moon was children
A dream escaping sorrow
A dream laughing in twilight shadow
With love alive
With hearts bleeding to strive
The moon was play
A dream dancing in twilight shadow

The sun was harsh
A scream reawakening memory
A scream of bitter color and light
So love unwrapping
So love's retracting embrace
The sun was harsh
A scream of bitter color and light

THE EYES OF MURDERED HEARTS

The eyes themselves shall be missed
Their brutal aqua-blue innocence
Thunderous eyes
The eyes of murdered hearts
Inconceivable eyes

But you have waited for this
How else does the world turn
If not with pity and fear
To be missed like stage lights
Shadows on weary roads
Eyes that are born and unborn

Those fierce angered eyes
Those boundless eyes
Death has made a god of thee
Perpetual eyes
How long you have withheld your love

BROKEN

Then there is this cutting
Staring with a host of unholy eyes
And a dark soul rising

She was dead on the tracks
I saw the imprints of many men
I remembered an untamed dog
A great lion roaring
And a falling red-orange sun
That played alive upon the sand
That soft and silky sea

Inside of us nature and nurture are afoot
In contest and harmony
In stillness and storm
Such that words remain pure
Like the pink tongues of angels' sons

In the winter of Jekyll and Hyde
This skin and bone of a woman
Pushed the aged and rotting curtains aside
What brokenness now could
Broken decide

THE WASTING

The curse of consciousness
Being the wasting
Horror of flesh alive with eyes closing

This can't be right
A world of infinite incongruous fact
A dark energy of negative reaction
Blood and the brain stems futile delight

We wake for a moment or think we awake
Improbable clump of dust and being
Covering our nakedness with sad believing
The mythic moon's mad mistake

Horror of wind and breath
Covering our skin with beautiful death

DEAR BUKOWSKI

Dear Bukowski I must leave you now
Yes it is over
I can no longer enter the bars for pitchers
Of green beer

I must use my own mind before it is too late
I have tried so hard to be you
Taking the heart of Los Angeles
To shred its soul

It is time to put your books on the shelf
It is time to leave
Your drunken nights in Hollywood
Your little fold out desk
Your little fold out chair
Your typewriter and your thesaurus
Which somehow held your memories of
Love and violence

Yes it is time
I thank you I thank your dead body in the
Ground or cremated I don't know
I must break from you by smashing the walls
It is not my fault
Your words were simple and sharp
You never apologized
I admired that

Goodbye my friend
Goodbye to all these photographs
I have held like golden Torahs
Hard to say goodbye after so many years
Hard to say farewell to those
Lonely nights where you saved me
And all those drunken and drugged nights
I have followed you home

The author

Philip Jay Marlin was born in Queens, NYC, on October 16, 1963 to Kenneth and Rebecca who had a short-lived marriage. His mother taught him to love art and words at an early age. She showed him how to paint with acrylics when he was ten. While in college in the late 1980s he was experimenting with writing song lyrics until an acquaintance gave him a copy of the slim volume of Whitman's 1855 version of Leaves of Grass. It was after this reading that he decided to devote himself to poetry. Soon after college he also began his visual art career. He now resides in Charlottesville, VA. He is an avid user of the poetry and art opportunities so numerous in this college town.

novum PUBLISHER FOR NEW AUTHORS

The publisher

> **He who stops getting better stops being good.**

This is the motto of novum publishing, and our focus is on finding new manuscripts, publishing them and offering long-term support to the authors.
Our publishing house was founded in 1997, and since then it has become THE expert for new authors and has won numerous awards.

Our editorial team will peruse each manuscript within a few weeks free of charge and without obligation.

You will find more information about
novum publishing and our books on the internet:

www.novumpublishing.com

Rate this book on our website!

www.novumpublishing.com

www.ingramcontent.com/pod-product-compliance
Lightning Source LLC
Chambersburg PA
CBHW030235170426
43201CB00006B/229